To every life traveller and those who want to
become one.

Live the present!

Foreword

In the early spring of 2013, I created a journey for my closest students to show them the secrets of the ultimate Knowledge through the Middle–East. I am not talking about the so-called Holy places, especially not those, who have been appointed by the modern, artificially created understanding of the 2 equilateral triangles. This view came into fashion long after the last turn of the Sun Ages in b.c.e. 3113 when Earth's consciousness was shaken and only the debris of the Philo-Sophia provided tangible memories to relate to and became the foundation of the future.

By her permanent appearance on the sky as a prominent member of the Haudi solar system the mysterious *Waiting for Venus* period has ended, and the five-pointed star became the symbol of Mystery, Knowledge, Hidden and Forbidden. The more evolved would look at her as the ambassador of peace, for it can only be achieved through understanding the Self and the high intelligence what wholeness would bring upon Earthlings. Others, with limited access into the abyss of the subconscious, where memories of the 22,000 odd years of Earthly living and valuable keys to the channels between the Micro and the Macrocosms are stored, would look for physical evidence and preach that only the touchable exists and everything else is the creation of Devil.

By denying the power of Knowledge, a new God was created that represented the surface, the physical strength, imperialism and ruthlessness. Rather cleverly this new God, the Materia or Money, was applied to the physical body and its pampering; convincing its followers that Nirvana comes to those who suffer emotionally and bear the understanding that money can buy happiness. It comes from the misconception that one's fulfilment is the straight result of the willingness and behaviour pattern of others. These new prophets would look at Venus as the cause for war against evolution and discovery of the essence in Earthly existence.

As always, the truth is in everything for it doesn't exist. In Islam the greeting *Assa'alamu Alejkum* means *I come with peace*. However not many remember that Salem, Salim, Salam, Shalom, and other similar words are the ancient name for Venus, the planet that still carries new experiences and unpredictable challenges with the comfort of the ever-lasting torch that leads Earthlings through awakenings and revolutions with a strong command for changes. Ur-al-Salim, the Courtyard of Venus, the Place of Knowledge and Peace slowly became Jerusalem; the centre of war and unhappiness, caused by the resentment for understanding and the denial of the fundamental law in The Universe, that all earthlings are equal.

Dancing with the Desertwolf

Life, my eternal love

Life traveller series

1st book

Zsa Zsa Tudos

AKIA

First Edition

Published by AKIA Publishing

Copyright © *Zsa Zsa Tudos 2019*

https://ex-files.org

zsazsa@ex-files.org

Cover photos: Zsa Zsa Tudos

1.

$\mathcal{I}$ am in no way an extraordinary person. Although I used to be a very nicely proportioned girl, years rounded me up a bit and put a special diet back on the table every now and then. I am not beautiful in a conventional way: I have a round, sort of heart-shaped face, big nose, small mouth but my eyes are really something. They are the greenest of green, quite sizable and always smiling. If it is true that eyes are the mirrors of the soul, the joy of existence is constantly in my eyes.

I love life. I adore its challenges, its joys and pains; its generosity and obstacles. I take every event as an exciting new phase and consider it a teaching of the highest level.

I was born into a very modest family in the South of Hungary. My parents were divorced long before getting married and I am certain they would not have gone through the trouble if I had not been on the way to catch the Light on Earth yet again.

I often wonder why I chose this family to descend into. It could have been the freedom of thoughts for nobody ever bothered with me. I was left to discover the farm, where I spent few years of my tender age on Earth with my grandparents; the forest next to it and the lake nearby, covered with thick vegetation and housed amazing wildlife. I befriended every insect, had conversations with the birds and talked to the trees. I gave them names of all kinds and occasionally we had meetings to discuss the events of the forest. Since nobody warned me I had no fear of anything. Now that I know more of the world I remember with a shiver that a cute viper used to be my playmate. Apart from occasional stings from bees and wasps my health and safety had never been violated by the residents of the enchanted woods. I lived a really great life there. Without overwhelming attention from grown-ups, my third eye stayed open and I was able to see, feel and live beyond earthly boundaries and the restrictions of the physical body. I went through star gateways and leaped into other dimensions easily without conscious awareness of the danger stored in the journey. I did not give it much thought and considering it my natural environment, I assumed that everybody shared my understanding of the world. I only became slightly suspicious when one day we were sitting around the big table in the kitchen, eagerly waiting for the result from the gypsy cards laid out by my grandmother. As the answer to her question about the watermelon harvest started to come through, she gazed at the window and said: "Mrs Veczo is here. And she is listening". Following the direction of her gaze, I saw a donkey under the tiny window that sampled the thick vegetation there.

"Funny name for a donkey!" I added smiling.

"What are you babbling about child? What donkey?" asked Granma surprized.

"There, under the window!" I was pointing to the friendly animal.

"There is nothing there, child!" she declared.

The donkey lifted his head, looked at me and I was certain I detected a faint smile in the corner of her mouth. "*Very clever of you Mrs Veczo*", I thought. Now that I am thinking of it, the donkey looked very similar to the Himalayan goat depicting the Devil, numbered XV in Crowley's deck. He is impish, irresistible, with power and self-confidence of a warrior and a definite winner. It came to me then that grown-ups might not be very knowledgeable after all. Later the idea became a conviction, and helped me leave behind certain events in my life with ease. Like when I did my entry exam to the State Institute of Classical Ballet. It was my mother's idea really. Usually, she did not pay attention to me but as many mothers, she always harboured a wish to see her offspring on a stage; even if it was myself. I was far her best bet, for my sister and brother from the second marriage did not walk on the same ground. Not because I was extremely talented but I turned out to be better than my siblings concerning fame and art. It came from my natural understanding that life is an enormous stage where every possible genre of plays is happening simultaneously, freshly written by time. On this platform we are interrelated shapers of the future, teaching each other valuable lessons and have great fun on the way. With this overwhelming perspective, I was very confident when I arrived at the Ballet Institute. My body structure is nothing like that of a ballet dancer. My limbs are not long enough for the purpose, my joints are not flexible and my thoughts are scattered. However, when a lady ushered me out of the big hall after my unsuccessful trial, I honestly believed that the decision was the loss of the Institute for they could not see my real talent. Although much later I managed to become a professional dancer after sixteen years of classical ballet, six years of jazz and some folk training, I have never been successful in the field. My relation to music and rhythm was very different from everybody else's. I identified with them and the people they

11

represented and I moved from my heart. I found it difficult to learn choreography. I was tall for a ballet dancer but short for any other fashionable rhythmic movement. As a result, I could not fit in a chorus and was not good enough to go solo. Nevertheless, the public enjoyed my performances; they loved and praised my talent and it landed me few solo dancing roles where I was allowed to use the music to my liking and mistakes could not be spotted.

The confusing status of my dance carrier helped mystify further my understanding of life, especially where relationships were concerned.

However against all my conscious work throughout the years to get somewhere in the performing world my success was only temporary in every field.

After his sudden appearance the donkey wasn't mentioned again. I saw him once in the forest, one morning chatting to an owl as I was passing through. We did not exchange words, only a wink of acknowledgement established the fact that our eyes met.

I loved the little farm where my grandparents lived. The two-roomed white-washed adobe house was the entire creation and work of the young couple arrived from the Far-Eastern part of the country to try their luck on the fertile land of Baranya county. The narrow front door led straight into the huge kitchen that also served as a bedroom for me and any other visitors happened to stay the night. At certain events such as the birthday-nameday of my grandfather, freshly stuffed straw mattresses covered the earthen floor of the room where we all slept after a long day of partying.

Peter Pal Toth was born on the 29th of June, on the calendar nameday of Peter and Paul. It was the date when grain harvest started all over the country. Before humanity messed up the weather, this day marked the beginning of various summer festivals. Being around the end of June-beginning of July full moon - that brings in the Fire festival of Litha at the Summer Solstice - the timing was perfect for an outdoor party. The forty days tropical rain spell coloured the sky clear blue and pushed the vegetation to grow. Freshly formed little animal and bird families were enjoying the caressing sunshine chatting about the wonderful things in life.

This particular day was very different from the rest. My grandma got up even earlier than usual to start baking those wonderful cakes and pastries to honour my grandfather on his special day. Soon the bread dough started to rise and graciously moved into the big clay oven built behind the house.

Grandpa Pal got out of bed at the crack of dawn. Like every other day, he fed the poultry first, after helped himself to a healthy breakfast of some home-made sausage, bread and raw onion. Then without further ado, he put on his better suit and a pair of comfortable shoes to set out for the nearest village, about 5 miles away, to pick up his usual order of fresh-river fish from the local fisherman. He actually happened to be Mr Veczo, the husband of the donkey under the window.

There were two beautiful horses in the stable by the names of Manci and Laci. Their main work was connected to the field and the carriage to transport us when it became absolutely necessary. However, we rarely took advantage of their power. We walked great distances those days. It was a way of life and good nourishment for the mind. The legs followed the path in the physical realm as we entered the Kingdom of The Ultimate Freedom of Thoughts.

This time of the year the early morning walk to Zalata was a fairy tale itself. The imminent arrival of the summer dawn was in the air. After a night-long hard work of cleansing and oxygen-producing, the trees turned in to have they well deserved peace and quiet while the rest of the organic population started a new cycle of life with rejuvenated force. The birds' choir launched a colourful hymn to send the Moon asleep and welcomed the magnificent fire globe in the sky. Although it was still dark, the accelerated motion and emotion added a high-frequency energy boost to the fuel of existence. By the time Grandpa Pal reached the end of the forest, morning arrived. The heat forced him to remove his jacket and roll up the sleeves of his freshly ironed white shirt. As far as I remember he only wore white shirts, even when out on the field. He pulled his hat deeper into his face as protection from the scorching sun. Pal was a fast walker. His lean body moved to the rhythm of life while his mind travelled freely beyond the boundaries of physical existence; over the rainbow.

Most of what I have in mind about my grandfather is imaginary. However, this image has changed as my consciousness developed throughout the years. As a child, I looked at him with awe and some sort of admiration blended with fear. He did not talk much, not to us anyway. Every word he uttered had a valid reason behind. We were continuously warned not to disturb his train of thoughts and behave ourselves, otherwise, we would become closely acquainted with his leather belt that held the trousers on his body. However, he was a sincere and just man. He was going on about his job to provide for the family. He usually stayed away from arguments and scolding children; left that for the woman folks. As I learned it later from my aunt Gizi, he was a real stallion and quite an entrepreneur all his life. At the age of 26, he had a hardware store of some kind that provided a decent income. Combined with his sexual power and good looks this fact made him a well sought after and eligible young man of his time. Grandma Ilona was a well-proportioned, good looking, innocent sixteen years old then, who was not afraid to walk an extra mile to reach the particular desire she had in mind. And Grandpa Pal was all she wanted.

Luckily he had 4 younger sisters who were happy to play part in Ilona's plot to lose her innocence to the desired man. With this event everything was settled: however, Pal had no desire to get married, for he was a revolutionary and he did not like the institution. He sold his shop instead, packed Ilona on a two horsed carriage and drove off into the sunset.

The possibility of a new life and the unknown excited him for he was ready to challenge his abilities all the time. The hardware store changed into tobacco and watermelon fields in his mind as he planned the next steps of life. With the first offspring on the way, and many more to come, it appeared to be a sound decision. On arrival at the South of Hungary he cautiously started searching for the perfect place. As he wasn't a socializing person he wanted a place away from the village with the possibility of self-sufficiency. Later it struck me that there were two other valid reasons behind his decision. Those days it was unprecedented to live in matrimony that is not holy by the understanding of the Church. Their first four children carried Grandma's maiden name. I also have the feeling that Grandpa did not like the Church for I had never seen him going there. Marriage as an institution came only about sixteen years later, when for reasons not revealed to me, Grandpa Pal walked to the nearest village and signed a piece of paper at the notary's office, according to which he officially wed his bride and the mother of his six living children. At this event, he acknowledged that he fathered all the children within the closest family circle. The other reason was Grandma Ilona herself. She was the socializing sort and liked to indulge in a little gossip here and there. Growing up with four younger sisters, Pal perfectly understood the danger of befriending people within the vicinity.

The farm he settled for was perfect in every way. It was easily reachable from the nearest village that housed about fifty families, but not close enough to make the journey in vain. The few acres of land was surrounded by forest from three sides while the lake fenced it from the fourth. There were 2 wells, providing clean, fresh, good quality water for men and animals alike. It was the last plot to the South, near river Drava that was the border between Hungary and big Yugoslavia. The young river was full of energy and playfulness with an abundant offer of nourishment; the wildlife in the forest was great too. Wild bores, hares and many flying species of the animal kingdom formed part of the great cycle of existence.

This wonderful sanctuary had only one little problem: there was no dwelling of any kind on the land. With the birth of the first child was fast approaching Pal needed to put a roof over the heads of his new family. A house on its own in the midst of wilderness needed the strength to withstand the ever-changing moods of the weather and the moist air coming from the lake. Under these circumstances, adobe bricks proved to be the strongest, cheapest and fastest way. With the help of a local gypsy they learned the craft, which beyond having the necessary shelter, provided additional income during many years to come. The little house was born and the family settled.

𝒯he walk to the village was usually the privilege of the children. They were not useful in the fields but strong enough to bring home the essential provisions the farm could not provide. However, today was Pal's day when his mind was free to wander without the constant nagging from his wife and the idle frictions and prickling from his daughters.

He enjoyed the freedom of thoughts; the power train that was capable of destroying the imprisonment of the physical realm, go beyond the realities of earthly existence and to extend this liberty yonder the alignment with his understanding of life in general.

Today he would go to the only pub of the small village to receive the best wishes from the folks, accompanied by some strong home-made palinka before heading home with a sackful of fresh fish, the main ingredient of the celebration dinner. The menu for this event didn't change throughout the years: fisherman's soup with tagliatelle pasta, fried fish and fish fillets in breadcrumbs accompanied by some chicken legs in breadcrumbs and potato puree. There was also a chocolate cake, a delicious pastry with poppy seed, the speciality of Grandma Ilona, palinka and plenty of good white wine to wash the food down.

By the time he arrived back to the farm, the bread was baked and the freshly made tagliatelle pasta was drying on the scorching sun. Four adolescent members of the poultry kingdom were sacrificed and neatly cut into portions, bathing in a special marinade that bought fame and respect for Ilona within the village circle. She was quite a cook, hard worker and compassionate. As a woman, she desired all-around attention, especially from Pal. When her wish wasn't fulfilled she sought recognition from her immediate family by following the strange practice of secretly playing her daughters against each other, and then invite herself to embody the role of the peace negotiator. This way everybody ended up happy and went to bed with great satisfaction.

When the Sun touched the crowns of the trees on the West end of the spacious garden, every member of the close family was accounted for; children to the couple who travelled from all over the country to honour their father enjoyed the meet-up and grandchildren were sharing stories and making plans for the summer togetherness. In the shade, under the old wall nut tree, the long wooden table was laid with a bleached-white hand-woven table cloth, adorned with two big-bellied demijohns sampling the best wine available in the region. By time, other bottles of less importance would join in as representatives of the finest home-made sweet liquors from Ilona's kitchen to please the ladies, and a tall-proud bottle of fine plum palinka to bring an appetite to the grown-up masculine members. Few steps away there was a long wooden board, supported by two chairs under it and covered with a patterned plastic sheet for protection. Five places were laid for the existing grandchildren. As far as I remember back we were always five. By the time the additional siblings grew up to participate in the event, I would have already moved away.

When I said that I spent my early childhood on the farm, it was more a wish than a reality. However, in my mind, the events in this enchanted world are only interrupted by moments of my other existence. They are like flashbacks, usually blended with some kind of violence and anger.

My mother, Margit was the second living child of Peter Pal and Ilona. Their initial aim for a son temporarily diminished by the birth of the first daughter but trying had never left the agenda. Despite his lean body, Pal was a fiery, sexually charged stallion, who needed daily intimacy from his wife. This reproductive urge resulted in numbers of premature birth and early death as part of rural family life. Since modern precautions were not accessible for villagers, the frailer gender invented and developed ways to help each other when unwanted pregnancies occurred. There was one particular lady in each village or in the vicinity to turn to in cases of fortune-telling, love-spells, tying knots, illnesses and offspring regulating issues. They would have been burnt in the Middle Ages when the Vatican launched a mission against everybody who happened to know more than allowed. Women were specifically targeted, in fear of messing up the male-focused Holy Trinity. However, the killing missions of World War II didn't reach the remote place and even after, in the communist era, the great majority of people remained in the flock of the Christian Church. Like it is today, it was a social force, fear banishing or convenience rather than conviction. During the mass only the so-called beautiful stories surfaced from the Bible, leaving the essence of the religion in the background. The widespread concept of the religion, according to which we are born sinners, only Jesus can heal and mortals should not interfere with the will of God were changed suitably to fit the demands of life without realizing that boundaries were stepped over and opened the place of make-pretence.

Although the couple didn't marry in front of God, all their children were christened to ease Ilona's mind about fitting into the etiquette of the village nearby. Thinking about it, I have only seen my grandma visit a church when invited to a wedding ceremony. Late in her life she followed my mother's conviction and joined the army of Jehovah's witnesses in favour of their views of everlasting existence and walking with lions. When she was taken to hospital at the age of 86, and she realized that it would be her final home, went silent and never uttered a word again. Ironically the village priest refused to bury her until a large sum was paid to save her lost soul.

Pal seemed to have a philosophy of his own. I do not clearly know what it was but I felt a strange connection with him. Similarly to myself, he didn't sulk or were angry long enough to affect his deeds or thoughts. He questioned things but never asked, for he provided adequate answers to his doubts. He was creative, persistent, a great enjoyer of life in his own way. He invented jobs where he could be alone and work independently in his spare time.

The fact that they lived in different dimensions, couldn't stop them to meet and agree upon family-related issues. One of the most significant subjects was the moral behaviour pattern of their five daughters. The dowry wasn't very substantial so the girls needed to make up for it by perfecting the rituals of essential household chores, such as cooking a clear chicken soup, making thread pasta that is not ashamed of its name, baking a bread that rises to the sky and stays there, create beautiful and tasty pastries, be at home in the garden and to give lives to healthy children.

Grandma Ilona served as a worthy example. Remembering back I had never seen her leisurely sitting down unless at a table with food on it or after dark when there was nothing more to do. The day ended by the Sun submerging into the wilderness of the lake.

The farm provided constant work for every member of the family. There was no electricity or any kind of machinery in the place. Tools, such as spade, hoe and scythe were driven by manpower with substantial help from the two horses when ploughing or transportation were concerned. After sunset, the Moon and the stars on the clear blue sky provided adequate light to listen to the crickets or having a conversation outside. When the weather did not permit, we sat around the kitchen table, munching some pastry, playing cards or listening to the battery run radio. The flickering beam of the petroleum lamp created moving shadows on the wall as an invitation for another world to open. We were always together but suddenly we started to live separate existences in a place, over the rainbow, where life conveyed different meanings. In my mind it was never better than what we had, only different. Now, that I know a lot about living in many dimensions, and the fact that good or bad do not exist, only within each other, makes me wonder about events in the little white-washed house.

Although later in their lives, they travelled miles, and moved from the corner of the country to the other one, in order to possess tillable land, in their youth the three eldest girls did not share the wonders and magic of the farm. They felt the restrictions implemented by Grandpa Pal on their skin, with the endless train of daily chores and the vague possibility of changes. Eligible lads in the nearby village were quickly picked up by the girls at hand, leaving the options provided by the small military base in the vicinity of the farm.

The enterprising aspect of Pal did not apply to his daughters. He had clear ideas about what the physically weaker gender needed as essentials for conquering life. Be good at household chores and make the husband happy, who in return would look after them. I think he was practical rather than sexist. Even higher education was free in the country with good state support. However, none of the girls excelled in any subjects and had never expressed the desire to pursue such a task. Therefore Pal took on the responsibility of keeping his precious offspring out of trouble.

The other half of the task landed on Ilona's shoulders. The girls, either willingly or forcefully, mastered thread pasta making, bread and pastry baking with all the delicate tricks of cooking under the supervision of their mother.

There was another story about my ancestors circulating among family members. It states, that Grandma Ilona hated Pal from the moment they met but a well-known sorcerer pushed the young girl into the arms of Grandpa. As a follower and practitioner of the Art, I know for a fact that even under the strongest spell you cannot keep doing things against your nature for a long time. The desire has to be in you somewhere to provide a hook for the force. Either way, they ended up together. My idea is that Ilona wanted to justify her constant complaining against Pal, therefore, she invented certain stories to clear the path.

After all those years I know that the real tyrant behind the scene was Grandma Ilona who desperately wanted to keep the peace, as she called it, between the five daughters. She had a very quaint perception of the word, for I cannot remember a day when all of them set at the same table due to sulking, anger or jealousy. Grandma Ilona was a very fine, laborious woman and a real manipulator.

I did not know my aunties much those days but today, with my widened horizon I look at them with horror. Five powerful cats, each with a sizeable doze of life elixir, chasing the morsels of happiness and satisfaction within the self - limited circle of existence, is a real killing machine. Grandma Ilona, faithful to her role as the leader of the female clan kept the fire burning at all times.

The eldest of the girls and Grandma's clear favourite was Ica, as she was addressed by the family and immediate friends. A petite woman with gentle features and a lean, well-proportioned body; she looked at the world as if she didn't belong. Very rarely smiled and had never danced or sung together with the others. There was a bitter – sadness on her face with a hint of disgust, as if she was constantly smelling poop. This expression was her shield; as for myself I don't remember ever conversing with her.

As the first-born daughter, Ica was meant for a good marriage with the best dowry the modest family could afford. She was hard working with good household skills; but above all, Ica was a dreamer and hoper more than a doer. I am certain she didn't know the very clever Arabic saying: *the man starts living when stops hoping.* She went on sulking when life didn't fulfil her hopes without doing anything about it.

Looking at her mother as an example, she befriended the sisters of the handsomest and richest eligible gentleman in the village of Zalata. The plan worked very well. She gained instant access to the village and the Szamek household without losing pride and dignity in the process. Ferenc, the gentleman in the centre of the story did not pay much attention to girly matters but his healthy attitude would allow him to observe the fleet of girls entering his sisters' lives. He was funny, witty and for the great joy of the females, he usually agreed when they begged for his company. Pique-niques, walks through the enchanted forest and swimming lessons in the river were carefully designed to bring the pair closer. Despite all the efforts his overall interest did not change and later shifted towards another pretty girl, with whom he married and lived happily – or otherwise - ever after.

However, Ica was so entangled in her dream world that she was convinced that her feelings were returned and the future looked very rosy. Until one day, when she paraded through the village accompanied by the sisters, they saw Mrs Szamek, the mother of the gentleman in question, sitting on a bench in the company of another lady from the village. After the necessary greetings, Ica heard her remarks: "She is beautiful, this Toth girl. Pity, she is poor." The sentence jerked her out of the pink cloud and brought her the realization that Prince Charming would never come to their farm to look for Cinderella. She didn't say anything but after bidding farewell to the sisters she disappeared from their lives. Soon after she agreed to marry an officer from the base who showed some interest in her.

Margit arrived into the family 3 years after Ica and straight away created quite a havoc. She was lively and strong-willed with resentment of Ilona's little attention being divided between the two daughters. Even later on, when every 3 years, like clockwork, an addition entered the family, she made sure to have what she desired and managed to cleverly redesign her role as the centre of attention.

However, one's desires mirror one's understanding of the possibilities and life itself.

The fertile land of the farm and its surroundings produced many wonders of nature that had always fascinated Margit. She dreamt about becoming an artist who colours an endless canvas with fragrances and substances of hues and shades. Cheap versions of the classics filtered into the household and filled up the little time between the twilight and bedtime. The flickering rays of the petroleum lamp took her through Stendhal, Dickens, Mora and Jokai. However, it wasn't the literary merit of these books that captured her. She was feeding on the storylines where lovers are united, cheaters punished, conventions ignored and the suffering of the heart derived from backgrounds of wealth, castles, beautiful dresses, servants and dinners. Although she was moved by the grief of the main characters, her desire focused on the wealth and the imagined flamboyance connected to it. The first step towards this aim was a valid plan to expand the microcosm she understood well and disliked so deeply. The hatred towards the land and the associated workload did not persist in later life but at that moment she only wanted to see the farm as a vague image from the past. The centre of the plan manifested in outsmarting Pal's watchful eyes. As a man of the world, he fully understood the urges of youth to copulate with everything that moves, especially when it comes in a pretty package like his offspring. Pal did not allow his daughters to meet anybody or anything in trousers out of his territory. Sisters were sent to spy on each other and encouraged to report suspicious moves. He knew that his girls need to make up for their dowry with the impeccable moral standard. He was also aware of the restlessness and stubbornness of Margit. Due to this factor, he showed some leniency towards suitors turning up at the doorstep. As for his daughter, she looked bored and somewhat disappointed when her mother called her name out to meet the interested party. She wanted a liaison who followed her wishes with adoration but was strong enough to look after her in every way possible. Someone who would take her away from there.

This unique desire cast a shadow over other events, logic and senses, landing exquisite colours to the only eligible gentleman frequenting the farm.

Jozsef was an army officer, in charge of the small border minding military unit of Haromfa, a tiny place nearby. He was of adequate height, could have been considered tall by a certain standard, had small, watery blue eyes and thin lips. The most prominent feature on his face was his quite sizable nose that I managed to inherit. He carried his well-built body with a certain pride without giving into emotions. Jozsef was a convincing talker and wasn't shy to use this ability on women around him. Since he wasn't in a particular hurry to settle down, Jozsef targeted married women in despair, who were longing for some kind of motion within the otherwise monotonous family life. Many of his lads were quite excited about the farm full of female presence, therefore at the end, he decided to check the situation out for himself.

2.

After going through the necessary visa procedures on arrival at Cairo international airport, my eight members group were met by a very nice guy called Ahmed. I was happy to see his smiling face for he impressed me with his efficiency and correctness in the past. Taking full advantage of his very limited English – mind you, I detected the sign of it being on the path towards improvement – he led us to a 9-seater *vintage* van. The confusion and disappointment must have shown on my face for he started to explain something about a garage and a lack of possibility; after which I arrived at the realization that the sixteen-seater comfortable minibus I was promised for the overnight journey to the ferry port of Taba on the Red sea, only existed in my thoughts.

I am always excited to see and feel something new. As I merge myself into the unknown so do I pull my students to experience, in the hope that they would not hold grudges, and after the initial fright, events will provide the base for funny stories during the years to come. Honestly, it doesn't always work out the way I plan; however they still refuse to travel without me. The highlight of my tours is the learning; and because there is very little overhead, they work out much cheaper than regular travel agency organized tours.

Our driver, also a nice guy called Mohammed, turned out to be very talkative. To crack a conversation he repeated the few English words in his dictionary over and over again, out of which I clearly recognized *OK* and *good*.

It was around 8 p. m. when we left the crowded city behind us and the scenery changed into a motionless sand-sea, broken only by scattered pyramid-shaped dunes. "*Funny how nature creates certain forms. As if it remembered the Great Pyramids of Giza*" I mused. The traffic on the road was just enough to keep our driver alert. Whenever opportunity allowed, he pushed the vehicle to its limit and gobbled up a big chunk of the distance. At first, he looked at me apologetically that he accompanied by few enthusiastic sentences. I listened eagerly, tried to catch the two familiar words in vain and this gave me a shiver of uncertainty. I only regained my fading confidence when I looked at the peaceful and trusting faces around me. And then I gave a broad smile to Mohammed through the mirror. As the night fell and everybody dozed off, I occupied my mind with planning the next few days ahead and also taking a turn or two on memory lane.

The first time I entered Jordan, was in 2003. Tourism to the country was flourishing with the backing of King Hussein and his Jordan Air. I had been staying in Budapest, Hungary semi-permanently for about 3 years at the time. There was my Church, a Pagan establishment where I taught my philosophy I named AKIA. I also worked in the most prominent esoteric healing centre as a healer and educator. To help my students I took advantage of my RSA/CTEFLA and ran intensive English courses solely for them for a small fee. One day when we talked about travelling, one of them mentioned a sign in a Travel Agency window; an exceptional offer for a week in Aqaba on the Red Sea. By the end of the session, seven of us signed up for the trip. It was the first of the many AKIA trips I still organize and run.

We arrived at Aqaba around two o'clock on a July morning. After passing through passport control we were escorted to a coach and taken straight to the hotel upon the hill overlooking the city. It was still dark outside, only the distant lights of Eilat on the other side of the Red sea and few scattered sparkling spots from the city broke the colour of the sky. By the time we filled the wardrobe with clothing and arranged the bed the clock turned 4.

Although we were up all night none of us wanted to sleep. The air was filled with a strange fragrance of the unknown and the mysterious desert nearby. The urge to discover some sort of secret overwhelmed us and we walked down the hill to experience the sunrise. The almighty fireball approached the city from beyond the mountain. Without the people the city's streets looked almost like any other Mediterranean place; square, white-washed houses with hanging electricity cables everywhere. Nevertheless, they were wider, more private and respectful. The curtains were drawn and we did not see laundry hanging on the balcony or windows.

Taxis started to circulate to let us know that their service was available when needed.

Suddenly a deep and soothing voice started to create an unrecognizable tune. Men, dressed in white long shirts merged and headed down the hill following the direction of the voice.

A gradual change in the movement of the car altered the course of my thoughts. As I looked through the window I saw a vast concrete land taken over from the mysterious desert. In the coach, everybody was sleeping peacefully cuddling the precious fresh water supply in a plastic bottle. Mohammed noticed that I was awake and it triggered him to start upon an explanation. This time I was helped by the road sign stating **Suez 20 km**. I smiled out of joy to be part of history and acknowledged the fact that the harder half of our journey was behind us. However when a couple of hours later I spotted a road sign **Sharm-El-Sheikh 280 km** confusion set in. A sudden urge took over to understand the situation, to know what was happening but since no valid explanation would have changed anything, it left with the same speed it arrived. The four large, plastic containers at the back of the car released a strong odour of petrol. The open window next to Mohammed was the only source of ventilation and allowed waves of fresh air in from the Sinai Peninsula. As I looked through the window next to me the sky was sharp dark blue and few constellations from the 22 star-formations zodiac clearly visible. There was the Majestic Moon in its waning state and following her Venus, looked brighter than ever. I always enjoy seeing the two majestic ladies up there. The Moon slowly but confidently moved on the path of learning by taking on new experiences; while Venus followed her impatiently cutting the distance between them. It gave me the feeling that she wanted to overtake the old lady in a haste. However, respect didn't allow it. So she kept her youthful pace shining brightly in the process.

On the road, the traffic was piling up around us. As the result, the car slowed down and at one point we arrived at a standstill. Soldiers were pacing amongst the vehicles as if looking for something. A precious 30 minutes passed by without movements when Mohammed got out of the car and walked away. He returned shortly accompanied by two uniformed men. They opened the side doors and greeted us cheerfully. Then looked at the piece of paper Mohammed handed to one of them, closed the door and started marching in front of us clearing the stationary traffic. Eventually, the road opened as we left miles of patiently waiting vehicles behind. Mohammed was very satisfied with his achievement. From his explanation, I understood that the road between Suez and Taba was closed due to the recent disturbance in Ismalia, and we needed to go around the Sinai Peninsula in order to catch the ferry to Aqaba, Jordan.

I adore this part of the planet. It offers me the clearest and deepest connection to Mother Earth. All the brainwashing and the so-called established man-made facts about the universe, the planet and humanity disappear, and allows me to look deeper into the past, present and future. Similarly to the centre of the dry land, the Giza plateau, this amazing architecture of nature carries the DNA of the world in the rocks, the sand and the sky. The Knowledge is not decodable by mere archaeology or other related sciences. Only with the help of inner vision and the depth of the subconscious. It would override the modern human approach with its fictional base that holds a sandcastle.

I am a curious and passionate traveller. I have seen all the manufactured wonders and the fingerprints of the Gods. However none of them is as awe-inspiring, cleansing, healing and helping as the land around the Step Pyramid of Saqqara, the Great Pyramids of Giza, the extraordinary dune and rock formations of the magnificent Sahara with its amazing wildlife, and the never-ending sand of Wadi Rum in the South of Jordan. They are great affirmations of the: *What is important is hidden* theory.

As I gazed through the window I discovered few members of the 22 star-formations. It was good to see them guiding us yet again, after four thousand odd years with the 12 members' zodiac that ended with the Quantum Leap on the 28th of December 2012. The sight started another train of thoughts in my mind. I saw Antoine Saint Exupery, sitting next to his broken airplane in the Sahara, under the immense star-studded sky and scribbling his thoughts into a notebook. For me,

The Little Prince holds many important keys to our past and our pretentiously gullible existence.

Suddenly my heart filled with excitement. An urge of pushing time took over. I could hardly wait to discover new wonders and feelings. However, it left at the same speed as it invaded me. A glance into the dark abyss of the universe through the window promised great stories and new experiences that couldn't be ignored.

A halt to the vehicle jerked me out of the philosophical mood. The next thing I noticed was Mohammed stepping out and circling the car with a troubled face. Looking further from the vehicle there was nothing and nobody around, even the road under us seemed to have vanished.

My watch showed 2.30 a.m. local time. We had 4 more hours to reach the port of Taba at the North-East part of the large finger of land. Closed eyes and deep sighs assured me that my companions were peacefully resting. I stood up, as much as the transportation machine allowed me to do so and slowly opened the door, primarily with the intent of letting some fresh air in. I climbed down the steps and turned away from the van.

$\mathcal{I}$ found myself in another dimension, on a planet yet to be discovered, where the cycle of nature is intact and untarnished by alien invaders such as humanity. My lungs graciously welcomed the high dosage of clear air to which I happily helped them, despite the slight dizziness the ozone - rich substance caused.

The unbroken sky presented an awesome view of the galaxy and beyond. The most prominent pair on the sky were the 2 Ladies: the Moon and Venus teasing and chasing each other along the horizon.

The abundance of twinkling stars created unrecognizable patterns of star formations. After spotting the densest flow of glitters, the Milky

Way, I transferred my attention to finding the enslaved princess of Andromeda. Her mother, Cassiopeia was nearby, with her shining W formation. My focus was shifted further and aimed at finding the second brightest object, Sirius. Following the Dog Star leads to the belt of the great hunter, Orion. They together played an important role in Egyptian knowledge and mysticism.

When I lowered them to the ground yet again, my eyes almost stopped functioning, due to the lack of light, giving way to the other, rarely used senses, such as ears, nose, tongue and skin. After the sky, the stillness of the ground felt like a heavy coat that covers the secrets and protects the lawful inhabitants of the peninsula. I heard the long-bearded goats jumping from one rock to another one, different types of rodents running around looking for food, and insects exchanging ideas when they paths crossing.

$\mathcal{I}$ felt as if somebody was looking at me from behind. I turned. My glance met a pair of deep and dark eyes that belonged to a fully armed soldier. He was standing still, trying to gauge my intention. Voices nearby broke my gaze. As I shifted my focus further, I noticed 2 white houses on the other side of the minibus, then I saw Mohammed in the company of 2 more members of the military force. I pulled my focus back to the person nearest to me. He sensed the questions piling up in my mind. Smiled, and with very broken English started to explain the situation. I learned that we ran out of petrol and although we had sufficient supply at the back of the vehicle, there was no means of transferring the liquid into the tank. I also understood that petrol was very difficult to come by, due to the sanction imposed on the country by the powers. He also mentioned that we were lucky to know someone such as Mohammed, who possessed enough of this treasure to take us to the destination we aimed for.

By the time we bid farewell to the helpful military checkpoint, it was 3.00 a.m. My companions were peacefully dozing and Mohammed seemed to be in control of the wheel. The fresh air, the stargazing and the countless journeys off memory lane totally worn me out. My eyelids were gaining weight on a fast scale and reached an uncontrollable state.

I don't know how long I stayed switched off. It must have been deep because I don't remember anything. I was at peace. Deep, deep peace. Until I felt a vigorous shake on my left shoulder. Suddenly I jerked out of my sleep. Opened my eyes and looked around frantically. My students were almost motionless in the most comfortable position they found on the narrow seats. The vehicle was moving ahead. And sideways...I looked at Mohammed. He was desperate to keep his eyes open and on the road. I said his name out loud and continued to talk. My watch showed 5 o'clock in the morning. I had no idea about our position on the road towards the place, where the ferry for Aqaba, was docked. I knew that it wasn't in the port of Taba. We had to look somewhere along the coast further up North. I continued talking to the driver, although it didn't develop into a conversation. However, my voice kept him awake and focused.

The Red Sea became more apparent on the left. The beautiful fireball emerged from the water, assuring a very hot and dry day ahead.

About 30 minutes passed by when Mohammed picked up the phone and dialled. In a short while, a white vehicle appeared, coming towards us, on the otherwise deserted road. Mohammed slowed down and allowed the car to turn around in front of us. He smiled as it led him to our destination. They all seemed excited by our arrival. The driver's expression showed joy and relief. Group members gathered the luggage quickly, while I paid Mohammed the agreed fee with a fat bonus added to it. He didn't even count the money, just watched us taken over by the next authority.

The boat was already filled with passengers, seemed to be waiting for our arrival. Three guys ushered us to the security check while another looked through our passports. We all went through the scan but Zoltan, the only male member of the group was stopped and asked to open his suitcase. To my surprise, they found a mint collection of chef's knives, carefully wrapped into a brand new, cotton kitchen towel. With my help, he started to explain to the shocked security, that we were planning to do barbeques on the trip and he thought, would be a good idea to make use of the beautiful birthday gift from his mother. By the time I finished my defence, the entire crew was around us, having a good time on Zoltan's naivety. Finally, the head of the establishment turned up and offered to take care of Zoltan's treasure until we return from Jordan.

I ran to Mohammed and gave him a final hug for the support and great work. He was a bit shocked but my action also brought a smile to his face.

I watched him standing there, in his not that crispy white shirt, smiling and looking at the boat to depart, and take us to new lands and new adventures.

3.

The long blond locks covered her shoulder creating a perfect frame for the slightly emphasized cheekbones and the big greenish eyes. It was Margit's favourite appearance after the day of chores placed on her by the household. The long, slightly gathered cotton skirt made an appearance accompanied by a white half-sleeved blouse. This picture always makes me think, for nobody in the family had blond hair. Throughout the years I even developed a suspicion that some kind of chemical was used, nevertheless up to the age of eighteen, when I saw my mother the last time, she was still blond.

This picture was convincing enough for Jozsef to develop some interest in the centre of his focus. Especially when he realized that Margit was more than willing to try the copulating game. His respect towards the head of the household held his urges back for a while however the golden locks, the freshness, the youth, blinded his better judgement and did what every man would under the circumstances. Since precaution wasn't widespread and definitely escaped the minds of these two, a couple of months later the story took an unexpected turn. I was created. The only trouble was that none of them were keen on having the product of their lust. Jozsef was happily playing the bee, polluting every flower on the roadside, and Margit dreamed about an imaginary place where FREEDOM is written with capital letters and individual wishes are granted without much ado.

Now that the future was in ashes, the present waited patiently to gauge the attention of the two culprits. Being the senior by almost a decade and a man of important official duties, Jozsef realized that the only remedy to the situation was marriage. He wasn't a particularly courageous person and this characteristic worsened through time. His biggest fear was to meet Pal face to face. Therefore he chose the noblest act possible: under the darkness of the night, he ran away with his new bride as far as the nearest village. There was a room in Mrs Legradi's house in Zalata, kept by the military for soldiers on leave, which served as a temporary abode for the growing unit.

Pal was on a killing mission for a few days that Jozsef managed to avoid with the help of his mates. The father of the bride gave up when he learned that it is all done, and the marriage certificate was signed.

After the first initial months following the event of properly introducing my lungs to fresh air, the crowded little room proved unbearable for the new family unit. Jozsef spent longer hours at work, so he said, and Margit became really unsatisfied with the outcome of her plot to escape the former family nest. It only added to their frustration that I came prematurely, and as all my relatives agreed upon, did not stop crying for the first 12 months of my earthly existence. In order to lengthen the distance between him and the angry-watchful eyes of Pal, Jozsef moved his family to a town called Mohacs, where he managed to secure a small army apartment on an estate.

It was around the time of moving when my annoying habit of crying disappeared from one minute to another, and for the amazement of all parties concerned, I started to talk. And from that moment on, I have never stopped. At a very tender age I learned endless verses about the animal kingdom, and stories of beautiful princesses who waited for the Prince Charming. Needless to say that behind those stories was my mother who hadn't given up the possibility, that one day it could still happen to her. These were the only occasions when she actually talked to me.

Or I should say, talked at me. I do not remember ever having a conversation with my mother. She said what she had to or desired to air. I realized early that talking to her was a waste of time and energy, so as far as she was concerned I kept my thoughts to myself. Not with other members of the public at large! I started early to give earthlings the benefit of the doubt, with a deep conviction that the same language spoken invites a similar understanding. Since I have always had a lot to say, there was no time to gauge the comprehension level of my audience. Apart from the renowned classic fairy tales I knew by heart, I followed the footsteps of Scheherazade and made up fascinating stories about far-away places. My fantasy ran wild in the uncontrolled environment. Nobody had ever checked up on me or my thoughts, and worrying grown-up faces didn't circle around whispering the fearful words: psychologist or crazy. Or if they did, I hadn't noticed.

The stories of 1001 Nights were great influencers of my day to day existence back then. My understanding was that we lived in parallel universes at the same time and one life supported the other existence through the lessons provided. Reality wasn't a question. It was set by the prevailing adventure in which I happened to take part. I do not recall mixing them in any way. I thrived on puzzles, unsolved situations and exciting exchanges of thoughts. When I think about it, I still do. I embrace the universe as a matrix, where events happen for reasons to further us on the road of evolving. In every answer I find a new question waiting to be tackled.

However, life would be boring without others in it. They provide influences, alter one's course of action and ways of thinking. Sometimes they try to connect with you peacefully and at others, jerk you out of your perfect little world with their harshness. My mother was the master of the latter. A frustrated young woman, who was left alone with a still needy small creature, with whom she had no time or intention to connect, let alone understand. Margit didn't take kindly to disturbances in her dreaming about some kind of recognition and the passionate love that only exists in the last sentence of most fairy tales: ...and they lived happily ever after. She needed conquests and emotional dramas on the big stage of Life Theatre.

The rail around the open French window of the room, which served as the bedroom for the family, was her favourite place to hang out; like a caged wild bird with a strong desire to fly but lacks the courage and the know-how to survive in the material filled environment. From the safety of the enclosure, she observed the neighbours passing by on their ways to the nearby bus stop, mothers taking their children to kindergarten on one corner of the estate or doing their daily shopping in the small supermarket on the other one. She was a pretty sight with her slender figure and long blond locks for the utter disapproval of the fairer gender.

However, males sent her satisfied glances often accompanied by a smile. She thrived on these moments. This narrow opening into different dimensions drew a never-ending yellow brick road into the abyss of existence, over the rainbow and into the city of the Wizard of Oz. As memory serves me, the only time my mother took me to cinema was years later to see Judy Garland as she fought against all odds in order to finally meet a person who guides her back to reality. It was the only thing Margit didn't like. Physical reality seemed to close the door she desperately wanted to keep open. It affected her to the point that she became violent and abusive when an event or a word, usually coming from me, shook her sandcastle.

There was one particular gentleman who caught Margit's eyes. He was a good looking married man known by the name of Mr Seres. I cannot recall his first name, I was around 3 years old at the time. His good look is really an assumption for in my memories he lives as a short, quite rounded, dark-haired person with a temper. Nevertheless, I would rather put the blame on my memory than my mother's choice of entertainment. However the latter part of the description was definitely true for Mrs Seres was keeping busy running up and down with a broom at hand, swearing and shouting, in an attempt to ketch the culprits in some kind of an act. The fact that she didn't succeed wasn't convincing enough to stop her from launching a punishing mission on Margit who temporarily gave up the much-loved position in the French window. I do not really know what exactly happened. Nonetheless, on one occasion, I noticed Mr Seres in our apartment wrestling with my mother. I must have said something, as the next thing, there was a pillow on my face.

$\mathcal{S}$ oon after that, events were accelerated and finalized in Jozsef moving his family to an army base on the nearby Southern border, where he was the officer in charge. We were housed in a 5 bedroom mansion that was abandoned by the owners when fled the country in fear of the communist regime. It was a beautiful house, as if stepped out of a fairy tale, surrounded by a mature park of colourful flowers, luscious bushes and trees.

Although he was nearer, I cannot recollect seeing my father more than before. On official occasions, he lined us up in front of fellow officers and soldiers but other than that we had little contact. These parades worked very well for both parties concerned. Jozsef was seen as a family guy with responsibilities, and Margit had the opportunity to conveniently show her pretty self to those in present. As the inevitable consequence, Eros wasn't shy to wound a tall, dark-haired and dark-eyed officer called Miklos Wolf and Margit. The only memory I have of this gentleman that he often amused me by turning my white dotted red ball on one of his fingers. When many years later he found me in London and we talked on the phone, I mentioned this to him. He couldn't recall the event.

I have no recollection of any event between the two of them, nevertheless, Miklos was soon replaced by a soldier, a young man with dark blonde hair, blue eyes and a smiley face. His name was Ferenc Rajli, a bricklayer by trade, from Tokaj, a town in the North-East part of the country. Ferenc was in the process of attending college to study architecture when he was called away for compulsory military duties.

Here is the place and time when I lost the thread. In reality, I'd almost lost everything.

In her spinning here and there, my mother paid less and less attention to me and my father wasn't around. It was autumn, the weather started to chill. I was often left in the house by myself. One day I fell ill with chickenpox that fast developed into scarlet fever. I was rushed into the nearest hospital in Mohacs where they diagnosed me with tuberculous meningitis and shook their head.

Despite the gloomy result, someone in charge ordered an emergency ambulance and rushed me to the better-equipped children's hospital in Pecs. Further tests showed even less promise. However being in the Communist era, luckily for me, medical treatments were free to everyone and the only goal was to cure the patient.

There were three wards next to each other on the corridor with huge windows between them. The third was the largest with 10 beds, the second was smaller with six beds and the last one had only 2 beds in it. I recall having someone on the other bed when I arrived; but very soon, I was the only person left in the room.

I have always adored and embraced life and protected it with my last breath. Remember standing in my bed singing a well-known folk song *I won't be here within a week* while doctors and nurses were looking at me with a sad expression on their faces murmuring *yes, she is not going to be here any longer.* But children capable of standing would wave at me through the window with a smile.

Needless to say, I prove them wrong. To the amazement of many, a week later they transferred me into the second ward and eventually, I became the resident of the third.

During the nine months stay I remember seeing my mother twice. I also recall that her belly was quite sizable at the last visit. I also saw grandma Ilona and aunt Gizi a few times. My father had never visited me.

It was around my sixth birthday when I was released from the hospital. I learned that Margit and Jozsef divorced, both got married, naturally to different people, and the new families produced an offspring each, while I was kept busy with the healing procedure. The divorce lawyer appointed Jozsef to be my lawful guardian. Nevertheless, he refused. Years later, my mother desperately wanted to find some kind of a home for me, other than the one she was staying in, and she ran out of relatives to approach, sent a note to my father and asked him to take me off her hands. Being totally faithful to himself Jozsef worked about 30 miles away from the home he shared with his already not that new wife and his spoiled little brat whom he only visited on weekends. So when Margit's note was delivered to the house, auntie Kato, a sizeable nursery teacher, received the envelope and was straight away intrigued by the letters on it. She was like an army officer: decisive, strong and no time waster. The letter was opened. I have no idea what was in it but every suggestion was pointing towards the fact that she had no prior knowledge of my existence.

There was also auntie Irma, Jozsef's sister, who was consulted about my placement during the divorce procedure. Strangely she developed some kind of liking towards me. However, she refused the responsibility, quoting problems in her marriage. Much later on, when I invited her to London, all expenses paid from my minimum wages that forced me to carry two jobs, she stated that I should not be ashamed of not getting anywhere and if she had raised me, I would have become an honest and respectful secretary by now, without time on my hands to find my path and dream about changing the universe. She added that I shouldn't have been ashamed of not getting anywhere in life.

It was the last time I saw her.

The freshly created family, Margit, Ferenc Rajli, Ferenc Rajli junior and myself as an addition, moved into a one-roomed shelter at the outskirt of Miskolc; a prominent industrial city on the North-West of the country. After finishing his compulsory military service, Ferenc was employed as a static engineer apprentice on a building site of a huge meat factory. There was an abode offered to employees without the nearby living arrangement for the duration of work. It was a long, one storey temporary building, divided into rooms, within which there was a coal-burning stove for cooking and keeping warm during the harsh winter, a table with 3 chairs, a wardrobe and in our case two single beds and a cot. A small aluminium basin kept under the table functioned as the washbowl where we took turns once a week. The room opened up directly to the narrow pavement which kept us out of the deep dust or sticky mud, whichever was produced by nature. At the far end of the building, two toilets serviced the natural needs of the inhabitants of the eight rooms.

My little brother was a very beautiful baby with his golden hair and big blue eyes. He could have stepped out of a fairy tale. My mother never let me near him while she was around. However, sometimes she needed to step out for this and that or go to the nearby little provision shop. Then I set down next to him and started telling all the stories I knew. Ferike was a good listener. Opened his eyes even wider and looked at me with a faint smile. My name is quite difficult to pronounce but as a token of his appreciation, it was the first word he learned. That is why I was a bit disappointed when one of the first sentences he formed was: *go to your father,* and pointed at me.

M y mother was warned by senior doctors not to enrol me to school straight away, in fear of lacking enough intelligence as the result of my illness. She did not listen. I must admit, it was her only deed that actually served me in the long run, even though it wasn't her intention.

The nearest school was about 2 miles away. There was no public transport of any kind in the vicinity. Personal vehicles were not widely in existence in those days. A narrow concrete road, leading to the city, passed near the building site, served as my everyday path to the establishment where I intended to learn about the world. Due to the lack of pavement, I walked the dirt on either side of the road. I assume there were no other school-aged children on the premises for I only remember taking the route solo.

I liked the walk. Even when the weather was harsh, I was happy to be out of the cage, away from Margit's reach, with my thoughts; usually humming a song, sometimes even burst into loud singing. Half of the journey went through fields, without any sign of human presence. There was a forest on the right side of the road, at the end of no-man's land, behind which the city started. When I reached the trees I stopped singing and looked out for the old forester who had been doing his morning round just about the time I was passing. Today it is very strange to think about, and difficult to imagine that during that time in Hungary people were employed by the state to look after vast groups of trees.

He lived in a small cottage with his wife at the farther edge of the forest. In the morning I was in a hurry to arrive at school by 7.45 but on my way home, sometimes our paths crossed and I was invited to homemade pastry served by the cheerful, always smiling lady.

I liked school. Even though my thoughts were running wild, discipline agreed with me, and also liked to use my brain. I was at the top of my class, specifically excelled in mathematics, physics, chemistry and literature throughout the years. I ran into trouble when boredom set in. Until today I need to be constantly entertained with fascinating projects, conversations, books, music or films. I like challenges and answer to deadlines well. School wasn't any different.

We changed homes a couple of times during the first 4 years of my education due to the demand of my stepfather's expertise. At one stage I remember having two rooms, all to ourselves.

I do not remember how it happened but one day, soon after finishing my fourth grade, I found myself on a train with my family, minus stepfather, heading towards the South.

We settled down in Baranya County, on the hillside of Terehegy, where Grandma Ilona and Grandpa Pal lived in a little house on the hilltop nearby. They gave up some of the inconveniences of the farm and the constant flooding of river Drava.

Our two-roomed cellar house with the vineyard, vegetable garden and variety of fruit trees stood majestically on 2 floors. It was an adobe house with 20 inches walls, small windows and a heavy iron door. The key to the house was about 15 inches long and weighed around 2 kilos of the same material. There was no running water or electricity in the vicinity. A latrine behind the house served our everyday needs. Despite these inconveniences, the house was clean and Margit kept it pretty. There were geraniums on the windowsill, net curtains on the windows and a colourful flower garden in the front.

The nearest community wheel well, around 500 metres away, offered the tastiest and the cleanest water I have ever sampled. For lighting, we used petroleum lamps. With the help of it, I prepared my homework and read the books I borrowed from the school's library. It wasn't fashionable for parents to help children with their studies those days. We used our brains and figured out solutions to exercises. There was no television, smartphone and digital games. We created our own games, played around and in nature.

Down the hill, there were scattered villages nearby. Every one of them had a small food store, where fresh bread was served 3 times a week, with all the necessary provisions villagers could not grow in the garden. Next to it, there was the drinking hole, where usually males gathered for a physical winding-down session after a long day work. Adjacent to the place was the culture hall, where films were screened, communal parties thrown, weddings and birthdays celebrated and dancing events held. There was the communal library, a small surgery for the general practitioner, who came to see the villagers once a week and another room serving as the school for the lower grade students. It was a pretty neat structure.

My fifth grade took me to the school in the nearest town Harkany, about 2 miles from my home. During the spring and autumn, I walked the distance on the dirt road leading to and through the village. There were two sisters, one of them my classmate, who lived further away, near the tiny railway stop. Usually, they took the train but sometimes they were adventurous enough to accompany me on the journey. When winter arrived, and the weather became wet and muddy, I joined them. There were occasions when due to the enormous snowfall and very low temperature, the train ceased working. Then we walked together on the top of the snow, through the fields.

My stepfather visited every now and then, and stayed for a few days. These were very strange times for me. They locked me out of the house for the whole day, usually without lunch and dinner, while the three of them supposedly had a good time together. I remember Grandma Ilona passing by casually sometimes and handing me a big slice of homemade bread with dripping to ease my hunger. I don't remember ever whining about my treatment. I was confused rather than angry. My little brother did not stop sending me to my father, my mother did not talk to me and I couldn't exchange words with my stepfather. So as far as I could see there was a unit and I did not belong to it. I stopped eating my favourite dishes due to my mother telling me that my disgusting father liked the same food. She conveniently forgot the fact that she loved them too.

School was going really well with me. My teachers discovered my love for poems and performing abilities, so I was given the honour of reciting the centre poem on every national holiday, some of them were connected to Communism and its achievements. I was still at the top of the class and my mother was only summoned once by my drawing teacher who complained about me humming a tune while concentrating on putting an image of an apple on the paper. She could've just asked me to stop humming.

By the beginning of the next school year, I was shoved to a strange house in Lakocsa, a village in the neighbouring Somogy County.

The residence belonged to Grandpa Pal's youngest sister called Bozsi and Jozsef, her husband; a childless couple in their late 50s. At the same address, there was a goat by the name of Zsuzsi, a sow called Sari, a dog Bodri, a cat Mici, few ducks, a dozen of geese and some chicken.

I was not aware of the negotiations resulted in my change of residence yet again. I went on with my everyday life of attending school, doing my homework, doing chores around the house, put the animals to pasture one by one. I learned to shell corn and weave beddings. First time in my life I had the opportunity to make friends who were allowed to come over to the residence of

Aunty Bozsi and Uncle Jozsef for a visit. It was also the place where I received the first May – tree from a secret admirer.

Well, nothing lasts forever. Near the end of the 6th grade school year, Uncle Jozsef died, as far as I understood, suddenly. This event ended my residence in the village.

I don't remember where I spent the summer but by the time the new school year started, I was taken to Harkany railway station with all my belonging. A quite robust, dark-haired and dark-eyed woman picked me up and accompanied me on the journey to fulfil my little brother's wish. She was taking me to my father. On the train, I learned that my companion was Auntie Kato, my father's wife. She was talking me to Vaskut, a sizeable village over the Danube.

Apart from my first experience with a fitted bathroom with an indoor toilet, Jozsef's home wasn't better than Margit's in any way whatsoever. By the time my 7th grade ended I was set to go back to my mother yet again. Soon after Jozsef and Kato divorced.

While I was away for two years, Margit and Ferenc junior moved back to the city of Miskolc, presumably to be nearer to Ferenc senior. This time they had a very small, two-roomed place in Diosgyor, the industrial area of the city. The first room served as a kitchen and dining area, while the second was furnished as a bedroom for the four of us. The limited space allowed only two single iron beds, one of which was for Margit and Ferenc, and the other one for my 5 years old brother and I. There was no bathroom; the shared toilets were located at the very end of the barrack.

For my 8th and final grades in elementary training, I was enrolled in a school nearby. Education in the country was centralized and quality controlled. All the fourteen subjects were taught in every school, and GCSE were compulsory in every one of them.

This was a very strenuous time. Margit and I had never stopped arguing, for nothing I did was good enough for her. There was nowhere to go and my final exams were coming up by the end of the school year. My hectic schedule was pushed further by the fact that I had to get up around 5 a.m., before anybody was even thinking about going to the toilet through the kitchen, because I needed the place for a major clean up. Every single night my little brother wetted the bed and I was soaked in urine. Added to the situation my mother and stepfather were openly arguing about me. I couldn't exactly fathom the main principle of the discussion however, I figured out that Margit was opposing me. Emotion was running high. We existed on top of each other in the cramped room, the four of us and Margit was pregnant again.

It was the only time in my life when I had meaningful conversations with Ferenc. He taught me the tricks of chess and gave me ideas for my mathematics' assignments. Both acts turned out to be very beneficial to me. I was selected into the school's chess team and brought in the city competition trophy. I was also giving demonstrations on multiplying three digits numbers by three digits numbers without aid, in my head, under 10 seconds. It was fun.

By law, education was compulsory until the age of sixteen, so I still had two more years to spend with it. Understanding my situation I pushed my mother to find me an apprenticeship, where I had the possibility to learn a trade and stand on my two feet. Naturally, she defied me. My grades were still high enough to get me into almost any school in the country. Since Margit's main incentive was *the further the better,* I ended up back in my birthplace, in the South of the country.

For the summer holiday, I was despatched to Tokaj, a very beautiful town where my stepfather's family lived. His mother, who I used to call Mamoka, was a sweet little lady. There was also the sister Mariska, a divorcee with a son, who was born from a later relationship, and there was Lajos, the older brother. It was a three-roomed house. The first served as the kitchen and the sleeping place for Mamoka, the second where I slept with Auntie Mariska and 4 years old son, also called Ferenc, and the third was for Uncle Lajos, the bachelor. The place was in a courtyard with 3 other families.

Beyond the back garden ran the playful and mysterious Bodrog River. On the shore, vegetation grew wild, creating a good place for conversations and pique-niques on hot summer days. It was also the place where I was kissed the first time at the age of fourteen.

Auntie Mariska commuted to Miskolc for work. One evening she mentioned that I should get ready in the morning for she will take me with her. During the years I got used to not asking questions, therefore I didn't.

I do not remember where I spent the day but after working hours I was united with my stepfather. He seemed very excited about our meeting and explained that Margit was in hospital giving birth and he thought it was a good idea to take me on a visit early morning tomorrow, in the hope of helping us to reconcile.

The two-roomed place, I remembered, was gone. There was one room with one single bed instead, with 4 chairs and a table. Ferenc put 3 chairs together and made a bed for me there. In the morning we were ready for the visit.

Entering the room one glance was enough to realize that Ferenc's plan badly backfired. Looking at me my mother burst into a rage which continued for few more minutes after a left the room. That day I learned that during the last 4 years the family was mainly surviving on the child support from my father and various state helps in order to put my stepfather's earning towards a quite luxurious house they were having built in an illustrious district of the city. The next day my sister was born.

I was taken back to Tokaj for 2 more weeks, until the end of the month, when the last journey, from the home I'd never had, took me to Pecs.

With the help of Auntie Gizi, my mother found me a room with a family of three. Uncle Gergely, the master of the household was around 60 years old and worked in the famous Zsolnay factory. Auntie Annus, with her 42 years, took odd cleaning jobs. Their son Istvan was around 5 at the time. According to the arrangement, they fed me, meaning that I ate what they cooked, they washed my clothing and gave me a private place to sleep and do my studies. I receive my father's child support and the allowance my stepfather collected from his work for my existence. After I paid my logging, there was very little money left for necessities, like school material and clothing. My whole wardrobe fitted into a small suitcase. I do not remember receiving gifts for Christmas, birthday or any other occasion. I used to pick up unwanted pieces, cut them to certain designs and create dresses I saw by hand. Later in life, this capability came quite handy when I enrolled in a fashion designing course at a London college.

I soon became a member of the family. It was for the best because the invitation to join any of my parents for the school holidays was lost on the post. For the 10 weeks of summer break my mother decided not to give me money for my up-keeping. She reasoned that I should take up some kind of work, and earn my living. During the first long pause, Uncle Gergely found me a job in the factory's packing department, where I had to carry piles of heavy porcelain plates from one place to another. I was a fragile-looking creature and only 15 years of age, therefore, after a week, the management sent me to the kitchen, where I cleaned potatoes for 5 hours.

Nobody visited me there. The only human interaction was my stepfather's letter he sent each month with a few encouraging words and a banknote. I usually thanked him and talked about my grades in school. He did mention that my mother shouldn't know about the letters.

I was very well into my second year, when one morning the school directress, Mrs Farkas knocked on the classroom door. She apologised to the teacher and called me out. She took me to her office, sat me down, and started questioning me about my family life. I told her that I could, after which she directed her enquiries to my stepfather and the relationship I had with him. At the time I couldn't figure out what the meeting was all about, nevertheless, I answered all the questions.

At the end of the conversation, Mrs Farkas looked deep into my eyes and said:

"Your mother is here. She claims that you had a sexual encounter with her husband. She wants us to terminate your studies. Come, we will see her together."

In the next room, there was my mother with two of my teachers. They all demanded answers from me. Mother said it happened when I was 14 and visited her in the hospital.

I was 16 at the time and still a virgin, so asked Margit to take me to a specialist but refused. She stormed out of the room. I went home totally perplexed. The next morning I didn't go to school. Few days after not showing my face at the premises Mrs Farkas came to see me with an assurance that I have my place waiting for me in the education system.

My mother came back once more when she told me that I was ugly and doesn't really matter what I do, I will end up being a prostitute.

Although I went back to finish my studies, from this moment on my life totally fell apart. I was forced to change accommodations a few times. In the process I arrived to the bitter realization that I was alone. Two years later I finished my advanced studies with 5 A levels. However, the naïve trust in humanity was tarnished.

4.

On arrival at our pre-booked hotel called El Qidra, I spent some time talking to the cheerful and exceptionally good looking staff while waiting for the rooms to be cleaned. I was anxious to book a short trip to Wadi Rum, the mysterious desert of the Bedouins, and show the magnificent sunset to my friends. The 2 taxi drivers that worked for the hotel, one of which looked like the Jordanian Antonio Banderas, were very helpful and I managed to seal a deal for 2 days later.

The western-influenced civilization of Aqaba shifted into long gone with the sight of the giant stone entrance to Wadi Rum. We stopped shorty at a half-fenced place where our newly appointed guide was leaning on the back of his white truck, in a pair of light brown trousers with matching leather jacket and a Jordanian scarf. As I stepped out of the leading taxi he greeted me with a broad smile that allowed his perfect teeth to be seen under the thick black moustache. Although I am not easily taken, his eyes captured me in the first instant. It was a blend of green, brown and yellow with an abyss of experience, knowledge and peace. He invited four people to share the driver's cabin with him and four to sit on the plateau of the small vehicle. I chose the fresh air and let the light breeze caress the scarf on my head. Looking back upon the road while moving forward, unveiled many secrets of the Hashemite land and the physical illusion of coming while going, offered a real treat to my senses.

Our first stop was one of the famous *supermarkets* where we were offered to purchase small hand-made souvenirs, while sampled a nice cup of spiced tea around the fire in the centre of the tent. I asked a few questions from the shopkeeper about his life and soon we set off to climb a fascinating rock formation. The smiling faced guide helped us on and off the rocks one by one, while I tried very hard not to look at him in an attempt to keep my fascination to myself.

The Sun was nearing the end of his daily routine. We climbed on the plateau of the jeep yet again to find the best scenery for the event. With the exit of the fireball, the air cooled down. The guide took his jacket off and threw it onto my lap with a serious face saying: "taste my scent". I was looking at it, mesmerized by his words, his courage and honesty. It conveyed strength and manliness. I didn't dear moving or touch the jacket for a while. And then, in my confusion, I offered it to the people around me in a hope that nobody would take it. I was relieved when I had the privilege of the wonderful male energy.

I set my camera up and waited for the right moment to catch the perfect sunset. He grabbed the opportunity presented by my stillness and stepped in front of me with a smile, removed his sunglasses and extended his right arm towards mines as if he wanted to remove them. The slow motion elevated my pulse. His powerful dark brown hand carried the playful promise of a tender-wild sexual encounter. I was very grateful when he stopped his hand about an inch away from my face; lowered his arm and slowly moved away. The fire within me accelerated until it became the Spring of Life, the creative power of anything is possible and everything is going to be all right. It was the World Peace and the Purpose of Existence. It was the Ultimate Freedom of Thoughts and the road to becoming four-dimensional. I wanted to preserve this precious feeling but my thoughts, man-made rules and scruples created boundaries slowly suffocated it and became diluted with shame. What if he is married? The thought ran through my mind accompanied by a bitter faint smile for I instantly realised that under the circumstances the question had no validity.

While I was pondering, a story came to my mind. When I received my refugee status in London, I was offered a rent-controlled apartment in Hackney, the land of Rod Stewart. Haha! The tiny, one bedroomed place was on the ground floor of a brand new building facing a pub and a funeral service office with a garage. Nevertheless, I was over the moon! I had never lived by myself. I'd always wanted to sink into the bathtub anytime and leave the dirty dishes in the kitchen if I didn't fancy washing them straight away. Not because I liked piling them up in the sink but because I could forget about them. Anyhow, there was a Turkish family opposite me. Nuten, the lady was in her late 30s, Turgai, the man of the household was a few years older and their daughter Yeshim was thirteen years old. Nuten was a dark-haired, sparkling blue-eyed, always smiling, and a pretty little woman. I'd never seen Turgai without a suit. His white shirt was freshly ironed all the time. He carried his slender figure with pride and his dark eyes demanded trust. I suspected that he was an educated man with a good job in his field prior to leaving his country. In London, he was a taxi driver. Yeshim was a happy and clever teenager. Sometimes Nuten called me over to sample her excellent cooking or just to have a chat, other times I let her taste the dishes I mastered in my brand new kitchen. She made a very good Turkish coffee, or Greek, or Arabic, depending on the country where you are enjoying it, and we arrived to the habit of reading the coffee grout when finished. She was extremely good at it, and I benefited from her teachings on the subject.

One day she came over with some freshly made coffee and delicious Turkish pastry. We sat down in my tiny living room laughing about trivial matters when she really cleverly changed the subject and started to talk about their lives as a family. She praised Turgai first of all, telling me how sensitive, caring and loving he was. And she was going on and on. I must admit I felt a bit of envy, for this is exactly what every woman wants.

I do not recall ever talking to her husband nevertheless her words made me curious. Then gently and intelligently Nuten turned the conversation towards a more private sphere of couplehood, sexuality. I couldn't detect any shame or confusion in her words, while she was explaining that her husband needs more intimacy than she does. Her lack of interest is caused by the physical pain she experiences during intercourse. Although I considered sexuality the essential aspect of life that was the moment when I started to feel a bit uncomfortable. Nuten did not stop. She went on explaining that it is a serious situation that led to a family meeting, where the 3 of them arrived at the decision to invite me into the family as Turgai's lover. His second wife if I wished.

I found myself lost for words. For one, I developed a Pavlovian reflex that was triggered by the word *married.* I guess to save myself from an undesired situation rather than respecting the piece of paper. On the other hand, I was deeply moved by her honesty, intelligence and the love for her husband.

Our friendship was tarnished. Soon I moved out of the apartment.

The natural role of the male as the physically stronger gender is clearly laid out in Islam. A male is ready to get married when earns enough to look after his wife and at least one future child. Without marriage sexual encounters are very limited therefore every male consciously works towards this goal. They gain inspiration from the family, the support of the wife and the rejuvenating power of sexual satisfaction. The strength of a male is in the number of his children. Should anything happen to the parents, children are continued to look after by relatives or the community.

Until recently, since the Islamic countries started to fall victims to the New World Order,

Consumerism and Globalization, there were no orphanages in the mentioned countries. Today prominent charities and charitable companies set up camps for children who lost their parents in the crusade. It feels as if Columbus was revisiting to demolish every bit of knowledge and dignity he accidentally missed half a millennium ago.

He noticed my withdrawal. A small bar of amber appeared from his pocket. He reached for my left hand, opened and rubbed it with the Bedouin perfume slightly above the wrist. Raised it to his nose, took a deep breath and gently released it.

"I am the desertwolf. I am a loner, I feel, smell, hear, taste and see. I am strong. I have five children. Dance with me!"

He pulled a man-made flute out of his pocket and started to follow the movement of the flickering Sun as it was bouncing on the sand. The rhythm nestled into my brain becoming a permanent guide. My fingers begin to touch the sand-filled air, running up and down in front of me as if I was hanging into the never-ending height of blue. "*How different the sky is in every country*", entered my mind. "*Here, it is a hue of a light blue, allowing the Sun to co-colour, and the desert to reflect back upon the countless hidden creatures.*" The shoulders eased up to extend the arms and dragged the hips with them. As I looked out I saw my companions joining in one by one. I continued to sway and turn gently that developed into an ecstatic celebration of Life, the Sun and the Land. I couldn't hear the sound of the flute any longer. The music came from within, perfectly co-existing with movements of the surrounding elements, with life, the only unconditional love available to us, earthlings. The wonders with their fragrances, substances, sounds, tastes, and welcoming appreciation.

LIFE, MY ETERNAL LOVE!

Other books from the author:

- **5 Secrets of the Matrix** – The true core of Self-development
- **Emotion the Machinery of Life** – The Missing Factors of Happy Relationships
- **Heavenly nourishment** – Conscious eating in 7 steps
- **Intersextion** – and they work together
- **The 4th Way** – Teaching the Gnostic Wisdom of AKIA Philosophy
- **Life is Yours to Win** – It All Happens in the Mind
- **Pandemic** – The story of mankind
- **The five minutes man and the girl who fell in love with mint**

Thank you very much for leaving a review!

Claim your free book here!

https://ex-files.org/gift/

Have a nice life!

www.ingramcontent.com/pod-product-compliance
Lightning Source LLC
LaVergne TN
LVHW041201080426
835511LV00006B/698